LEGENDS AN
OF LONDON

Pollyanna Jones

BRADWELL
BOOKS

Published by Bradwell Books

9 Orgreave Close Sheffield S13 9NP

Email: books@bradwellbooks.co.uk

British Library Cataloguing in Publication Data: a catalogue record for
this book is available from the British Library.

1st Edition

ISBN: 9781912060689

Design by: Andrew Caffrey

Typesetting by: Mark Titterton

Print: Gomer Press, Llandysul, Ceredigion SA44 4JL

Photograph Credits: iStock and credited individually

CONTENTS

INTRODUCTION

Old London Town

London has captivated hearts and imaginations through lore and literature for centuries. Still lovingly referred to as 'The Big Smoke', it evokes images of crowded, bustling streets, lively with the cries of market-stall owners, buildings stained black with soot, and Dickensian charm. Popular culture paints the city as a progressive yet quaint city, smart and quintessentially English in nature, with costermongers selling fruit on street corners, paperboys calling out headlines of the latest news, and old women selling bags of seed to feed the pigeons of Trafalgar Square. In reality, London is a city filled with surprises, each district having its own distinct feel. From the grandeur of Westminster to the urban edginess of Tower Hamlets, every district meets you with pride and a distinction from its neighbour. Every district has its own history and tales to tell.

London has influenced culture and literature greatly, but is a very different beast to the city it once was or the stereotypes that we might imagine. It is a city that straddles the meridian line from which the hours of the world are measured. It is a city of wealth and promise, calling to men like Dick Whittington to seek their fortune. It is a city of shining towers, art and culture, music halls and theatres. It is a city of cut-throats and thieves, of smugglers and witches. It is a city of heroes, great minds and establishments, where ancient guilds still to this day are represented through the companies representing various trades.

London is a city that finds its own riches through the swirling stew of the people that dwell within it, both British born and from nations around the world. It has always been a melting pot of cultures, from Roman days and possibly before. It is in London where these people meet, share their stories and make new ones of their own through the histories they forge.

Delve a little deeper, peer beyond the glass-fronted skyscrapers, and you will discover that London still holds many secrets and gems for you to discover. Throughout the city, plaques can be seen naming the sites of events such as the bakery on Pudding Lane where the Great Fire of London started in 1666, or the homes of alchemists and astrologers like William Lilly, who studied his arcane crafts on The Strand and through his divinations predicted the Great Fire itself.

Beneath your feet, ancient ruins lie, remnants of a Roman city razed to the ground by an enraged Queen Boudica of the Iceni tribe. All about, the city speaks to you, sharing its stories. All one has to do is pause from the commotion of the busy streets, and listen. From legends of King Arthur and ancient Britain, to superstitions and witchcraft, giants, legend and myth dwell here still in this, England's capital city.

Scala paſſuum s pedum.
80 160 240 320 400 480

ON

Spitle fertides.

Botolp

Aldgate

Eaſt Smithfild

S. Belſins gate   *Galley kaye*   *The tower*   *S. Katherynts*
iren kaye   *Cuſtom howſe*

fluuius.

S. Towleyes

S. Marye Ouerys

LONDON'S MYTHICAL ORIGINS

'O powerful goddess, terror of the forest glades, yet hope of the wild woodlands, you who have the power to go in orbit through the airy heavens and the halls of hell, pronounce a judgement which concerns the earth. Tell me which lands you wish us to inhabit. Tell me of a safe dwelling-place where I am to worship you down the ages, and where, to the chanting of maidens, I shall dedicate temples to you.'

So was spoken the prayer by Brutus of Troy, legendary descendant of Aeneas, who is described by Geoffrey of Monmouth in his 12th Century work, *Historia Regium Britanniae (History of the Kings of Britain)* as being the first king of Britain. First appearing in an anonymous 9th Century piece called *Historia Britonum*, Geoffrey elaborated on the legend of Brutus, who gathered to him a group of enslaved Trojans and after becoming their leader, sought a new land which they might call home.

During the voyage, Brutus and his followers came upon an uninhabited island named Leogetia. Swathed in forest, the island appeared to be uninhabited, save birds and beasts, yet echoes of its past were revealed to an exploration party as they traversed the isle. In a glade deep within the woods, they came upon an abandoned temple devoted to the Diana, which contained within a statue of the goddess herself which miraculously answered any questions asked of it. Brutus made haste to the sacred spot, taking with him a group of his most trusted men where the hero performed a rite with three sacrificial hearths to Jupiter, Mercury, and Diana. With a cup of sacrificial wine mixed with the blood of a white hind, Brutus uttered prayers before asking Diana for her guidance in discovering a land which he and the Trojans might call home. Pouring his cup of wine upon Diana's sacred hearth, Brutus lay out the skin of the white hind before the statue of the goddess and settled down upon it, where he fell into a deep slumber. In the silvery realm of dreams, Diana herself whispered to him of a promised land.

'Brutus, beyond the setting of the sun, past the realms of Gaul, there lies an island in the sea, once occupied by giants. Now it is empty and ready for your folk. Down the years this will provide an abode suited to you and to your people; and for your descendants it will be a second Troy. A race of kings will be born there from your stock and the round circle of whole earth will be subject to them.'

And so Brutus set sail to the west with his men to the mysterious land described by the goddess Diana. Passing the north coast of Africa, they made their way to the Pillars of Hercules. Here they met with Sirens who with their enchanting song and terrible powers nearly sank the ships in a maelstrom of dark magic and seductive calls. After averting disaster, Brutus made the decision to drop anchor so that the voyagers could rest and replenish their provisions. It was during this stop that they met Corineus, whom after the kingdom of Cornwall would be named, who joined the fleet to discover New Troy.

After weeks at sea, the Trojans finally reached the prophesised land, stepping foot on the shores somewhere near a town we now call Totnes, located in modern-day Devon. The land was at this point, known as Albion and was as described by Diana, completely uninhabited save for a race of giants. Barbaric and simple, the giants were soon defeated by Brutus and his forces who drove the them into the mountains. Brutus chose to name the island Britain, and called his companions the Britons, after his own name so that they might be remembered down the long lines of history.

Brutus decided that in order for his kingdom to be established, a capital must be created. He scoured the land until finding the perfect spot, he built his city on the banks of the River Thames, naming it Troia Nova, or New Troy. Brutus took with him two captured and tamed giants who were known as Gog and Magog, who were chained outside his palace to serve as the city's guardians.

*Depiction of the statues of Gog and Magog, from F.W. Fairholt, Gog and Magog: The Giants in Guildhall: Their Real and Legendary History, **London: John Camden Hotten, 1859**.*
Public domain

Gog and Magog during the Lord Mayor's Show, 2006.
Photograph by S. Pakhrin, Public domain

Statues were later crafted to remind Londoners of their ever watchful protectors, and still they may be seen walking amongst men as they stride along the procession during the Lord Mayor's show each November.

Whilst the legend of Brutus and Troia Nova sets a certain grandeur for the history of ancient Britain and the founding of London as the nation's capital, it is unlikely that there was a city on the site of modern London until around 43AD with the coming of the Romans under Claudian's invasion. History may be clouded by legend, yet the legacy of the myth of Brutus is still felt throughout the capital to this day.

THE LONDON STONE

Few artefacts in the city carry such weight of legend as a small block of oolitic limestone known as the London Stone. Dating at least to the days of Roman Londinium, stories attached to the relic link it to many legends from the Druids to King Arthur. This little-known landmark has survived centuries of turbulence; from Viking raids to the Blitz, with superstition decreeing that the success of London depends on the survival of this rock.

Geoffrey of Monmouth described in his 12th Century, *Historia Regium Britanniae*, of how the city's legendary founder, Brutus of Troy brought the stone base of a statue of Pallas Athena along

The London Stone, seen through its protective grille in Cannon Street in 2004.
Photo by 'Lonpicman', Wikimedia Creative Commons, public domain

with him on his quest to seek *Troia Nova*, or 'New Troy'. Guided by Diana to Britain, Brutus erected a temple to the goddess in thanks for her guidance, and laid the blessed stone within it, upon which ancient kings of Britain would swear oaths to serve him. This legend was taken up by the Reverend Richard Williams Morgan, who wrote in *Notes and Queries*, published in 1862, how:

> 'So long as the Stone of Brutus is safe, so long will London flourish'.

This superstition has stuck, and despite fire, war, and development leaving an impact on the city, the London Stone has been kept safe from harm.

There is no doubt that the London stone is of a great age, and it is thought that it was part of a Roman building, possibly the provincial governor's palace, although it could have been a Roman '*milliarium*'; the central milestone from which the Romans would measure distances across their British province, much in the manner that we measure Longitude from the Prime Meridian in Greenwich. There may be some significance in the stone's use as a boundary marker, as it was situated in the centre of a grid of streets laid out when the Anglo-Saxon King Alfred re-built London in 886 following a series of devastating attacks by Viking raiders which had destroyed much of the old city. Known in Old English as the *Lundene Stane*, it earned the name by which we call it today.

It is said that kings and queens of Britain would visit the London Stone as part of the ceremonies leading up to their coronation and strike the stone to denote that they are the rightful heir of Britain, with King Arthur himself having associations with this intriguing rock. We see the first appearance of the legend of the sword in the stone in the early medieval manuscript *Merlin* by Robert de Boron.

According to de Boron, England had fallen into chaos following the death of King Uther Pendragon. Our heroes Arthur, Kay, and his father Entor, had met with the wizard Merlin at Christmas in Logres, where the nations great and good were striving to decide upon Britain's next king:

'The archbishop sang mass as far as the gospel; and then, just as they had made the offering, and day began to break, a great square block of stone and an anvil appeared, and in the anvil was fixed a sword. Those who beheld this wonder ran to the church to tell the people; and the archbishop came out bearing holy water and precious relics, and he went and saw the stone and sprinkled it with holy water. Then he noticed what was written on the sword: that whoever could draw the sword from the stone would be king by the choice of Jesus Christ.'

The legend of the Sword in the Stone was picked up by Sir Thomas Malory in *Le Morte d'Arthur*:

> 'And when matins and the first mass was done,
>
> there was seen in the churchyard, against the high altar,
>
> a great stone four square, like unto a marble stone;
>
> and in midst thereof was like an anvil of steel a foot on high,
>
> and therein stuck a fair sword naked by the point,
>
> and letters there were written in gold about the sword that said thus:--
>
> Whoso pulleth out this sword of this stone and anvil, is rightwise king
>
> born of all England.'

Malory narrowed down the location of the stone to being on the site of the greatest church of London, speculated to be the site of St. Paul's Cathedral. Interestingly enough, the long-term resting spot of the London Stone at 111 Cannon Street is less than half a mile to the west from St. Paul's.

Arthurian legend describes how the young Arthur drew the sword from the stone during a contest held during the feast of Christmas, proving through divine intervention that he was the true king of England, and it seems the 25th of December is a special day for the London Stone. Its dedicated resting place is mere yards from the site of a Roman temple dedicated to Mithras, whose day of birth also fell on 25th December. This date also matches the ancient Roman festival of

Wood engraving illustration by Gustave Doré of The London Stone, from London: A Pilgrimage, *by William Blanchard, 1872.*

Public domain

Dies Natalis Solis Invicti, meaning 'the birthday of the unconquered sun' a festival celebrating the rebirth of the sun after the darkness of winter, allowed the use of the title *Sol Invictus* for several solar deities to be worshipped collectively.

Not all legends attribute the London Stone with noble virtue. Britain's histories are often spiced with grim and macabre tales, and the London Stone was described by John Strype in his 1720 *Survey of London* that the stone was 'an Object, or Monument, of Heathen Worship' and was set in place by the ancient Druids who used it in their rites. This was further embellished by William Blake in his epic poem *Jerusalem:*

They groan'd aloud on London Stone,
They groan'd aloud on Tyburn's Brook:
Albion gave his deadly groan,
And all the Atlantic mountains shook

This elaborate description of human sacrifice popularised the idea that the London Stone was a sacrificial altar, and legend grew of the relic having a dark past. Folklorist George Laurence Gomme described in the late 19th Century how the London Stone was London's 'fetish stone' to which offerings were given once a year. The Lord Mayor of London is the latest in the long chain of 'chiefs' of the city to whom this responsibility had fallen upon, for in keeping the London Stone safe, the city itself will flourish.

The London Stone, in the Museum of London, 2017.
Photo by Pollyanna Jones, used with permission

DICK WHITTINGTON

Perhaps the most famous of all of London's Lord Mayors is Dick Whittington. A familiar and much loved fairy tale, '*Dick Whittington and His Cat*' is the story of the rise of a humble country boy to one of the most powerful men in England. It contains the message that London is a city in where dreams can be made true as long as one works hard, and never give up hope.

The story begins by explaining how Dick Whittington was orphaned when he was very young, so never knew who his mother and father were, nor where he was born. The child spent his days wandering the country in rags scraping an existence, until one day he met with a wagoner who was travelling to London. Dick asked if he might go along with him as he had never seen the great city, and the wagoner eventually agreed.

The lad was greatly excited by the prospect of seeing the city said to have streets paved with gold, but his hopes turned to disappointment when upon his arrival he saw that the streets were covered rather with dirt. Cold, hungry, and without a penny to his name, Dick asked the people of London for charity, yet only found harsh words and curses in return. After a bad run of luck, he eventually found employment at the house of a merchant named Mr. Fitzwarren who offered him work as an assistant to his cook, and offered him an attic room.

Unfortunately, the cook was cruel and would often beat Whittington, and his draughty accommodation was infested with rats and mice. The poor lad suffered sleepless nights until after cleaning a visitor's shoes, he was offered one penny which he invested in a cat. His companion provided valuable friendship, and cleared his attic room of the vermin that for so long disturbed his sleep.

A day came when the merchant gathered his servants, declaring that he was soon to send a ship out to trade. An opportunity for the house staff to earn themselves some wealth, it was a custom for them to offer something to their master who might sell it whilst abroad at a profit. Each servant came forth with an item to offer. With nothing to his name but his cat, Dick reluctantly offered Puss to the merchant, who sent the mouser off to sea.

Heartbroken Whittington decided that he would run away. He snuck off one morning, whereupon reaching Holloway, he found a stone and sat upon it to consider where he might go. Had it been a terrible mistake to seek his fortune in London? Should he return to the countryside? As he was pondering his next course of action, the bells of St. Mary-le-Bow begun to ring, Whittington thought that they were singing,

"Turn again, Whittington, Thrice Lord Mayor of London."

Dreams filled his mind of how he might be dressed in velvet and ermine, riding aboard a fine gilded coach through the city. He then resolved to return to the merchant's house and get back to his duties before anyone noticed that he was missing.

Meanwhile, hundreds of miles away, Puss and the trade expedition were blown off course by a storm. Dropping anchor off the coast of Africa, they arrived at a land inhabited by the Moors. Invited to trade, they were led to the King's palace, where to their horror, observed that the beautiful city was infested by rats. The King and his court could not even enjoy a dinner without the rodents boldly scampering across their platters.

Statue of Dick Whittington and His Cat, Guildhall, by Elisa Rolle, 2013.
Public domain

Statue of Dick Whittington's Cat on Highgate Hill.
Photo by Duncan Harris. Public domain

The plague was so dreadful that King offered a great deal of treasure to anyone who could relieve them of the vermin. At this, the captain sensed an opportunity and sent for the ship's cat which Dick Whittington had so nobly offered for the voyage. Upon arriving at the palace, Puss leapt into action and killed a great number of rats, causing the remainder to flee. The King was overjoyed and declared that he had to have that cat at any cost, offering the captain ten times the value of the goods already sold in exchange for Puss. A bargain was struck. Puss made the Moor King's palace her new home, and the ship was laden with so much gold and treasure that her hold heaved.

Illustration from The Story of Dick Whittington, **Heart of Oak Books**, *1906.*
Public domain

The good ship Unicorn set a return course for London, and upon arriving, the tale Puss was explained to the merchant. Dick Whittington was sent for to break the news that he was no longer a servant, but a gentleman of great fortune. Fitted in the clothes of a gentleman, his face washed, and hair curled, he made a handsome fellow, and the merchant's daughter Miss Alice fell in love with him. Fitzwarren gave the pair his blessing and the two were married, settling into a fine house of their own and establishing their own family.

The humble beginnings and hardships endured by Dick Whittington made him into a fine and compassionate man. He served as Sherriff of London, was three times Lord Mayor, and was knighted by the Queen. He made sure that his wealth benefited those less fortunate than he, and took care to give charity to feed the poor. He built a church and a collage, with a scholarship fund for poor students. He also had a hospital built to tend to the sick. A great man and great philanthropist, Dick Whittington lived a long and happy life, wealthy in more ways than gold could ever provide, for a kind heart shall never be poor.

Dick Whittington was in fact a real person. Born in the late 1350s in Pauntley, Gloucestershire, Richard Whittington was not a poor orphan as the story tells, but rather the third son of a local landowner named Sir William Whittington. Not expecting to receive any inheritance, he set out to London in around 1370 to make his fortune and make a name for himself. Initially gaining an apprenticeship with the Mercers' Company, he eventually became a very successful merchant himself, dealing in valuable cloth, and was appointed the Master of the Company several times. He carefully built up a network of influential customers such as Robert de Vere, who was a favourite of King Richard II, and by 1389 Whittington was dealing with the King himself, supplying cloth of gold to for the Royal wardrobe, earning enough wealth to be able to lend money to the Crown, resulting in power and influence. King Richard II appointed Whittington with the role of Mayor of London, which he served four times, not three as the story implies. His influence continued into the reign of King Henry IV, who sought his advice on many matters.

Upon his death in 1423, Richard Whittington made sure that his devotions to the good of the city would not die with him. He left around £5,000 worth of assets to be used for charitable purposes. Buried alongside his wife in St. Michael Paternoster Church on College Hill, the famous Lord Mayor was it seems, not destined to rest in peace as his grave was disturbed several times. John Stow wrote in his 1598 *Survey of London* that he was buried three times:

> 'First by his executors under a fair monument; then in the reign of Edward VI, the parson of that church, thinking some great riches, as he said, to be buried with him, caused his monument to be broken, his body to be spoiled in his leaden sheet, and again the second time to be buried; and in the reign of Queen Mary the parishioners were forced to take him up, to lap him in lead as afore, to bury him the third time, and to place his monument, or the like, over him again, which remaineth, and so he resteth.'

During repairs to the church in the Twentieth Century, the remains of a cat were discovered. This led to a frenzy of excitement about how Dick Whittington's cat had been found. If the tale is anything to go by, of course it is not, for Puss ended up in Morocco.

It is theorised that the mummified cat had possibly been sealed in alive behind the stonework by superstitious builders of the day. As the passage in which the cat was found had not been opened since 1691 when the church was built, it may well have been put there by a mason when Wren's church was being built to ensure good luck or to deter rats and mice.

Replica drawing of Richard Whittington by Reginold Elstrack (1570–1625), from Samuel Lysons, The Model Merchant of The Middle Ages, *1860.*

The Fitzwilliam Museum, Public Domain

WITCHES AND ALCHEMISTS

Throughout the history of England, the powers of witches, wizards and warlocks have captured the imagination and instilled fear into god-fearing Christian folk of the realm. As the capital city, London has more than its fair share of stories of spells being woven and curses flung to be rid of an enemy.

The earliest documented account that we have of witchcraft in London dates from the year 948, and was recorded by the monks of Peterborough Abbey. England at this time was under Anglo-Saxon rule. One of these, a thegn by the name of Ælfsige, had undergone a falling out with a widow who had inherited an estate after her husband's death. Ailsworth in what is now modern-day Cambridgeshire was a small but bountiful estate and while it is not known what started all the trouble, we can certainly guess! A complaint was raised by the thegn, who accused the widow of using witchcraft in attempt to cause harm against him by crafting a doll in his likeness before stabbing it through with an iron needle. The effigy was allegedly discovered in the widow's cupboard and she was formally charged with witchcraft, and sent with her son to London to stand trial before the good King Eadred. In the presence of the Saxon king and his court of abbots, bishops, ealdormen and thegns, the widow was tried for her alleged crime.

Trial by reputation was the order of the day, and the call was given for those loyal to the widow to give evidence that she was of good character. With the serious accusations against her, none would risk their reputations by siding with a so-called witch, and the widow and her son were left to the mercy of God to decide their fate. Choosing 'trial by water', the accused were taken to London Bridge to be thrown into the River Thames. If they drowned, then God would deem them guilty. If they floated, then they were truly innocent and would be spared. Unfortunately for the widow, her accusers were taking no chances. She was bound tightly before being flung into the murky waters. Her son managed to escape by running away; clearly a sign of guilt! While the widow died, he was declared an outlaw, and the estate of Ailsworth was gifted to thegn Ælfsige as compensation.

Cases of effigies made in a person's likeness were a seemingly popular way to cast a curse upon one's enemy, and a popular way of creating such a thing was by shaping a piece of beeswax to represent the intended victim. Prince and pauper alike feared the dark powers, and there are plenty of examples in London's history of witches standing accused of creating their dolls for personal grudges, political causes or simple payment. Even a witch had to earn a living!

The royals of England were particularly concerned by these wicked deeds. Supernatural forces were at work to usurp the throne, with the royal household employing their own mystical agents to protect them against their enemies. Ill-wishing and curses could bring sickness, afflictions, death and bad fortune, and as the king or queen was protected by God, only those practising the dark arts could possibly bring any unexpected ill events upon the good and the great of England.

In the 16th and 17th centuries there was much interest in the occult arts as a science, with astrologers and magicians practising divinations through the form of communing with angels or other forces, often with a crystal and maybe a black mirror: a round piece of smoky glass which they would gaze into and commune with spirits. While women were persecuted for conducting such rites, men such as William Lilly, a Leicestershire-born farmer's son, would travel to London to seek out their fortune. Taking up a servant's position, he married his former master's widow and took up the study of astrology, publishing *Christian Astrology* in 1644. Described as the 'English Merlin', Lilly was hugely influential with his advice to politicians and lords of the day with his charts and divinations.

Lilly's work was not without its controversy. Among other events he was said to have predicted the Great Fire of London of 1666. Published in 1652, his chart has been subject to study in recent

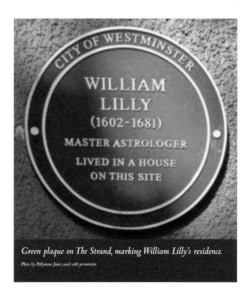

Green plaque on The Strand, marking William Lilly's residence.
Photo by Pollyanna Jones, used with permission

times, suggesting that not only did Lilly correctly guess the year, but also the date and time through astrological characters represented in his drawing. Modern-day astrologer Maurice McCann studied Lilly's drawing, with its astrological characters

Lilly's hieroglyph predicting the Great Fire of London, from Monarchy or No Monarchy in England, *1652.*

From the Museum of London

represented by people, before placing them on a chart to decipher Lilly's hieroglyphic code. From this, McCann deduced that 'We may therefore infer that Lilly predicted that the time of the blaze would be about 5.26am on the 2nd September 1666.'

So alarming was this prediction that after the terrible event which claimed so many lives, Lilly was called to stand before a committee who were to deduce whether Lilly himself had been involved in causing the blaze that had started on Pudding Lane. After much scrutiny, Lilly was finally dismissed and no further allegations were made against him regarding the tragedy.

John Dee's 'Four Castle Disc', crafted as a magical tool based on a vision from his seer, Edward Kelley.

Photo by Pollyanna Jones, used with permission

Lilly was not the only famous astrologer of London. Perhaps the best known of these men was Dr John Dee, a great mathematician, astrologer and occult philosopher. Serving Queen Elizabeth I as an advisor, and advocating England's creation of a British Empire, he saw no conflict between the arts of science and magic, using divination, alchemy and Hermetic philosophy to assist and protect the Crown and England. He had amassed one of the greatest libraries in England, and with the help of his seer, Edward Kelley, developed his famous Enochian language, claimed to be the celestial speech of angels. Born in 1527 in London's Tower Ward, Dee enjoyed much renown until Queen Elizabeth's death, and was so well known that it is believed he was the inspiration for the sorcerer Prospero in William Shakespeare's *The Tempest*. Dee died in 1608 or 1609, leaving a great legacy and influence on those to come after him.

Portrait of John Dee.
Public domain

Portrait of 'Mother Damnable, a Witch' from the Wellcome Trust.
Public domain

Black dog folklore is fairly common around Britain, usually with the apparition being the damned soul of one who had been wicked in life, cursed to take this form in death and never find rest. One such creature was said to haunt old Newgate Prison and was believed to be the ghost of a scholar who had used black magic to curse and harm his victims, who was later devoured by starving prisoners within the prison. First described in 1596 by Luke Hutton, a pamphlet of 1638 describes how the beast stalked the prison to exact terror upon the inmates:

> *'Amongst many others cast into this Denne of misery, there was a certain Scholler brought thither upon suspition of Conjuring, and that he by Charmes and devilish Witchcrafts had done much hurt to the King's subjects, which Scholler, mauger [in spite of] his Devils, Furies, Spirits and Goblins, was by the famished prisoners eaten up, and deemed passing good meat. This being done, such an idle conceit possessed the minds of the poore Prisoners, that they supposed nightly to see the Scholler in the shape of a black Dog walking up and downe the Prison, ready with his ravening Jawes to tear out their Bowels, for his late human flesh they had so hungerly eaten.'*

The Borough of Camden, and more specifically Kentish Town, is home to the World's End pub, once called The Old Mother Redcap. Dating from at least 1745, this pub has a legend to tell about the woman from whom it acquired its name. According to Samuel Palmer in his 1870 *History of St Pancras,* The Old Mother Redcap was named after a character known as 'Mother Damnable, the remarkable Shrew of Kentish Town'. Palmer identified this woman as Jinney Bingham, the daughter of a brickmaker named Jacob and a Scottish pedlar woman. Both parents were tried for witchcraft for allegedly causing the death of a maiden through practice of their black art, and were hanged for their crime. Jinney paired up with Gypsy George Coulter and had his child, who was later hanged for stealing sheep. Jenny then moved in with a man named Darby who was known for his drunkenness. This fellow mysteriously disappeared without a trace shortly before Jinney moved in with a man called Pitcher, who was later found burned to a crisp in his oven. A neighbour testified that the man would often hide in the oven to evade her sharp tongue, and it would seem that this time, to his misfortune, it was in use. Following this alarming death, Jinney withdrew from the public eye and kept herself to herself. Times were hard, and so she took in a lodger, who — no surprises — also died under sudden and suspicious circumstances, with rumours abounding that Jinney had poisoned him.

As age withered her looks, Jinney was often the target of angry mobs who accused her of being a witch. It is stated by Palmer that the Devil entered her house to take her. He was never witnessed to leave, but upon investigating her abode the following morning, Jinney was found dead before her fireplace, with a teapot full of herbs, drugs and liquid. This concoction seemed to be further evidence of her evil powers, as when it was tested on her cat the poor animal lost all of its fur two hours after, and then died. Jinney's body was so stiff with fright when they found it that the undertaker was obliged to break her limbs in order to place her in her coffin. Whether there is any truth in Jinney's reputation we cannot say for certain, although it was believed she had a talent for prophecy and she was compared to the more famous Mother Shipton in this poem from 1676, now kept in the British Museum:

'Y' have often seen (from Oxford Tipling house),

Th' Effigies of Shipton fac'd Mother Louse,

Whose petty pranks, (though some they might excel)

With this old Trot's ne'er Gallop'd Parallel.

'Tis Mother Damnable! That Monstrous thing,

Unmatcht by Mackbeth's Wayward-Womens Ring

For Cursing, Scolding, Fuming, flinging Fire

I' th' Face of Madam, Lord Knight, Gent, Cit, 'Squire'

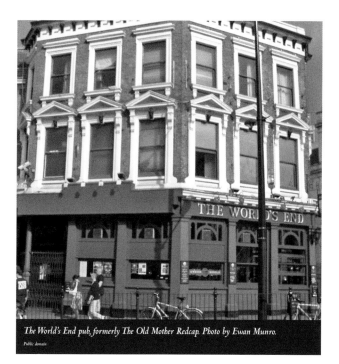

The World's End pub, formerly The Old Mother Redcap. Photo by Ewan Munro.
Public domain

Evidence of foul play through witchcraft was discovered in Lincoln's Inn, Camden, in 1899, where a cursing square, made from lead, was found. Laid as a curse to smite the career of a certain Ralph Scrope, it was hidden in the building to ensure, according to the inscription, 'That nothinge maye prosper nor goe forward that Raufe Scrope taketh in hande'. Scrope was associated with the building between 1543 and 1572, placing the square in Dee's period, and it utilised a prescribed system as detailed in Henry Cornelius Agrippa's *Books of Occult Philosophy*, published in 1651. An inscription against the chosen target was made on one side, with a numerical grid on the other, to ensure the curse's effectiveness. It would seem that the person laying this particular curse, however, was not well practised in magic as mistakes were made in the numerical square. Scrope enjoyed a successful career, becoming one of the Inn's governors. The practice of inscribing curses on lead has ancient origins, with such items being discovered from Roman times, imploring the gods to punish certain citizens as vengeance for their wrongdoing against the petitioner.

Many such items have been found throughout London, demonstrating a widely held belief in the effectiveness of concealed items as an effective method to achieve a result through supernatural forces. A popular method was that of the witch bottle, whereby items would be placed inside a glass or clay container, to be sealed and hidden while it did its work. At Paul's Pier Wharf in the City District, a witch bottle was discovered containing a felt heart stuck through with

five brass pins. At the site of Holywell Priory near Bishopsgate, another was found during construction of the East London Line, containing around sixty copper pins, nails, and a piece of wood or bone, under the floor of an 18th-century building. While we could assume that these items might have been used to curse, it is believed that they have more to do with defensive magic, being created to turn an ill-wisher's curse against them. These items were very popular in Elizabethan times, with several discovered hidden beneath fireplaces, or the furthermost corner of a house, with the intent that they might catch any evil directed towards those that dwelt within.

The use of charms and curios has not lost its appeal through the ages. As recently as the First World War, it was not uncommon for young men making their way to battle to be given a 'lucky mascot' to keep them safe from harm. Edward Lovett described in his 1925 book, *Magic in Modern London,* that a woman hid a small carnelian pendant into the lining of the tunic of her only son. It is said that her son returned from the war without a scratch. Lovett was a collector of curious objects and wrote extensively of his finds, which included the front feet of a mole, which when carried would be used as a cure for cramp, and small stones with a natural hole through them which were thought to be lucky. Lovett emphasises that these 'must not be looked for, asked for, or bought'.

Besides alchemy and witchcraft, another arm of the supernatural was catered for by Gypsies and fortune tellers who sold charms and read fortunes, and performed minor feats of magic for a fee. Steve Round in *London Lore* gives details of an article that featured in *The Times* newspaper of 29 March 1825, from the City of Westminster district. A £10 note had gone missing, and a fortune teller was called in to discover its whereabouts:

'A few days ago, a woman of colour, named Elizabeth Dodd, was brought to this office upon charge of fortune telling. It appeared that a woman named Mary Edmonds, living as cook in the family of Mr Prendergast, MP, in Berkeley square, had a sum of money given to her by Mrs Prendergast, to pay the butcher, baker, &c.; this sum consisted of five £10 notes...'

The cook somehow lost one of the £10 notes, which in those days was a great deal of money. It would appear that all efforts to locate it were in vain, for she then called upon the services of 'a very high character of the dark-coloured prophetess' who had a great reputation and record of success in finding lost items. A ceremony was performed in the Prendergast house, then the prophetess took out a key and a Bible to perform a spell to find the thief. In a common technique, a house key would be placed within a Bible which was then bound tight shut, before being passed from person to person. The key would be placed within the pages containing a certain verse, for example Psalm 50:18, 'When thou sawest a thief', and the book would twitch when passed to the thief and be placed in their hands to signify their guilt.

Using this technique, the fortune teller divined that the money had been taken by the nursery-nurse, a young woman named Susan Watkins. Disturbed by what had been undertaken by this woman under her master's roof, and denying all knowledge of the missing money, Watkins summoned a police constable to attend. The 'witching-woman' was arrested and tried and was sent by the Magistrate to a House of Correction for a duration of two months, but alas, the superstitious cook was convinced by her divination and the poor nursery-maid was dismissed from service.

Steve Round gives another example of dishonest fortune tellers from Frying Pan Alley in Tower Hamlets, 1816, relating to a woman named Harriet Garva, who earned a living making bonnets but supplemented her income through the telling of fortunes. A table spoon, a teaspoon, and four dessert spoons had gone missing from the house of the father of Elizabeth Shunstone, who on interrogating her niece, Charlotte Anthony, discovered that Charlotte had taken them to Harriet. Elizabeth then went to see Garva under the ruse of having her fortune told. It was during this fortune telling that Garva had the audacity to divine how Elizabeth had had some items stolen, and described her niece as the thief. Confident that she had all the evidence required, Elizabeth reported Garva to the constabulary, and she found herself before the Old Bailey who convicted her of receiving stolen property and ordered her to be transported for fourteen years.

BRIDGES OF LONDON

The city of London is split through the middle by the mighty River Thames, its murky saline waters influenced by the tides. This made the city very wealthy thanks to the merchants and visitors from afar bringing goods and money to London. Once, London Bridge was the only main thoroughfare into the city, with ferrymen operating a lucrative business taking passengers up and down and across the river. It was not until the coming of the age of steam that more bridges appeared, to allow trains and eventually motor cars to cross the Thames. Over time, numerous bridges were erected over the span to make it easier for the city folk to traverse the capital.

London Bridge

London Bridge has been the site of a bridge crossing the Thames since Roman times, with a timber bridge spanning the river from the fortification of Londinium on the north side of the Thames to the marshy south bank. Thought to have been built in around the middle of the first century AD and traversing the river from what is now Lower Thames Street to Tooley Street on the south bank, this makes it the site of London's most ancient crossing. Naturally, with so much history behind it, so too are many tales told about this famous bridge, most commonly associated with the nursery rhyme, 'London Bridge is Falling Down':

London Bridge is falling down,
Falling down, falling down,
London Bridge is falling down,
My fair lady.

Build it up with wood and clay,
Wood and clay, wood and clay,
Build it up with wood and clay,
My fair lady.

Wood and clay will wash away,
Wash away, wash away,
Wood and clay will wash away,
My fair lady.

Build it up with bricks and mortar,
Bricks and mortar, bricks and mortar,
Build it up with bricks and mortar,
My fair lady.

Bricks and mortar will not stay,
Will not stay, will not stay,
Bricks and mortar will not stay,
My fair lady.

Build it up with iron and steel,
Iron and steel, iron and steel,
Build it up with iron and steel,
My fair lady.

Iron and steel will bend and bow,
Bend and bow, bend and bow,
Iron and steel will bend and bow,
My fair lady.

Build it up with silver and gold,
Silver and gold, silver and gold,
Build it up with silver and gold,
My fair lady.

Silver and gold will be stolen away,
Stolen away, stolen away,
Silver and gold will be stolen away,
My fair lady.

Set a man to watch all night,
Watch all night, watch all night,
Set a man to watch all night,
My fair lady.

Suppose the man should fall asleep,

Fall asleep, fall asleep,

Suppose the man should fall asleep?

My fair lady.

Give him a pipe to smoke all night,
Smoke all night, smoke all night,
Give him a pipe to smoke all night,
My fair lady.

Like a lot of nursery rhymes, this song has origins in historical events. Many early histories were passed down verbally through story or song, and the tale of London Bridge is no exception. The first bridge at this crossing we constructed from wood and clay, and may well have been washed away during a flooding event. It was later fortified or even rebuilt with stronger materials to withstand the powerful tidal currents of the Thames, and later suffered at the hands of Vikings when the Norsemen came to London in the 11th century. The bridge was destroyed, and so to secure the city and prevent so easy a passage into London, a stronger version complete with drawbridge was constructed to help stop unwanted visitors entering the city. The stone bridge was completed in 1176 after 33 years of construction. Designed by Peter de Colechurch, it consisted of twenty arches with towers and gates at either end. It even had a watermill which used the strong current to grind grain. By the turn of the 14th century, the bridge was heaving with shops that thrived on the custom of those coming in and out of the city. It is thought that the silver and gold referred to in the nursery rhyme is a reference to this.

Thanks to the arches at the base of the bridge, the Thames would become treacherous as it flowed swiftly through them. The waters were concentrated as the river passed through the arches, causing fast-flowing currents and swirling eddies. At certain times of the day when the tide was turning it is said that the river levels could vary in height by as much as two metres from one side to the other, making a passage under the bridge as dangerous as navigating a vessel through rapids, which became known as 'shooting the bridge'. Many accidents occurred at this point, with countless lives lost to the Thames' angry waters. In a bid to ensure safe passage through at this point, certain bargemen on approaching the bridge would utter 'Gord bless Lon'on Bridge; Lon'on Bridge never did I any harm'. This would be repeated until they passed safely to the other side, upon which they would turn to the bridge and exclaim, 'Damn an' blast thee Lon'on Bridge!' according to John Emslie in *London Studies* (1974).

One particular myth about London Bridge is a rather eerie one, telling how screams are carried on the wind from the river. There

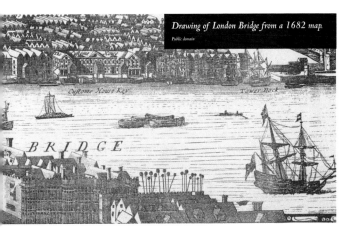

Drawing of London Bridge from a 1682 map.
Public domain

are two explanations provided for these spectral cries, the first of which relates to the dangerous waters.

In the late 13th century there were tensions between Christians and Jews in England. The Church had forbidden money-lending for profit, a business which the Jews practised, applying interest to their loans. The Jewish community became highly unpopular and subject to persecution until the situation reached boiling point when in 1290 the Jewish population was expelled from England on pain of death by King Edward I. Hundreds of Jews had boarded a ship moored near London Bridge to be carried to safety from England, taking with them all their worldly possessions. It is said that the ship somehow sank into the river, with all souls perishing in the disaster. According to Chris Roberts, who recorded the legend in *Cross River Traffic* (2005), their cries are allegedly heard on still nights from the embankment near to the Customs House.

Another explanation of these spectral screams is related to the heads of traitors displayed on London Bridge. It was the practice between 1305 and 1660 that those executed for treason would have their severed heads dipped in tar before being exhibited on spikes or stakes along the bridge as a deterrent to any would-be villains. The haunting sounds of their cries are said to warn would-be traitors of their fate should they go forth with their plans of treason against England and the Crown.

London has a reputation for making fortunes, although not all are to be found directly in the city. The legend of the Swaffham Pedlar describes how a fellow made his way to London following a particularly vivid dream in which he met someone who would tell him some joyful news. He found the place that he had seen in his dream: a spot on London Bridge. Upon reaching the bridge, he watched passers-by bustling about their business. Eventually, after three whole days, a shopkeeper came out to see what he was doing, loitering there so for such time. The pedlar explained that a dream had inspired him to make this journey, upon which the shopkeeper laughed at him. He chided him for his journey, saying how he had dreamt himself of a great treasure buried under a particular oak tree which stood in an orchard in a faraway town called Swaffham, yet he knew that dreams are nonsense so had not left London in search of such a place. The pedlar listened carefully and thanked him for his advice. As soon as the shopkeeper made his way back into his store, the man turned about and quickly returned home, where he dug under the tree described in by the shopkeeper's dream and found a pot filled with gold.

Putney Bridge

The second bridge to be built crossing the Thames, Putney Bridge was opened for use in 1729. It links the districts of Putney at the south to Fulham at the north, and is said to be the only bridge

Putney Bridge by J. Farington, 1793.
Public domain

in England to have a church at either end, with St Mary's at the south and All Saints Church at its north end. According to folklore, Putney Bridge was erected by a very frustrated Sir Robert Walpole. Later becoming Britain's first Prime Minister, Walpole and his servant were on their way from Kingston-on-Thames to the House of Commons. Walpole had just met with King George I to discuss some rather urgent business and needed to relay this to Parliament. Reaching the riverside, Walpole was dismayed to see that the ferry boat was on the other side of the Thames. They called the ferryman, but their cries were unheard as the man was sitting in the Swan enjoying a few tankards and could not hear the waiting passengers across the river. Forced to take another route, Walpole angrily swore that a bridge would replace the ferry to prevent such an inconvenience happening again.

Tower Bridge

Built between 1886 and 1894, Tower Bridge is an iconic landmark. With its impressive towers and ornate stonework, it straddles the Thames with a working drawbridge; bascules are opened to let larger ships pass along the river, then lowered to restore passage to road vehicles when the vessel is through. Ghostly tales are linked to this magnificent structure which was once home to a morgue in the base of the northern tower. Boats would moor at the landing to offload bodies for burial. Reputedly haunted by the ghost of the man who designed it, Sir Horace Jones, Tower Bridge is a reputed hotspot of paranormal activity. There are accounts of the sound of footsteps, and whistling in the Engine Room with visitors reporting the chilling feeling of being watched, being physically pushed or having their clothing pulled. Sir Horace died in 1887 and never lived to see his work completed, yet his spirit lingers on.

Tower Bridge, closed for traffic, 1900.

Public domain

Cannon Street Railway Bridge

Completed in 1866, this bridge was originally named the Alexandra Bridge in honour of the Danish wife of future king, Edward VII, and was designed to cater for steam trains crossing the Thames to Cannon Street Station. Sited near the location of the London Stone, Cannon Street takes its name from Old English, *Candelwrichstrete*, meaning a street of candle makers. This fell within Candlewick, one of London's old wards. Candles were of vital importance to a world without electricity, and in older times candle-leaping was both a sport and a form of fortune telling. The nursery rhyme endures to illustrate this old practice;

> *Jack be nimble,*
> *Jack be quick,*
> *Jack jump over the candlestick.*

Participants would chant the rhyme while leaping over a candle for luck. If the flame was not extinguished, good luck would be granted for the next twelve months. This practice is recorded as taking place on St Catherine's Day, 25 November, and was once widespread across much of England, perhaps harking back to older pagan rites of leaping over a bonfire.

Southwark Bridge

Originally a toll bridge, Southwark Bridge is named after *Suthringa geweorche* or *Suthriganaweorc*, meaning something along the lines of 'the defensive works of the men of the south' in Old English, indicating the Anglo-Saxon heritage of this London Borough. Comprising cast-iron spans mounted on iron pillars, the bridge has featured in many films including *Harry Potter and the Order of the Phoenix*. The bridge also plays a part as 'the Iron Bridge' in *Our Mutual Friend* and *Little Dorrit* by Charles Dickens, with mention of

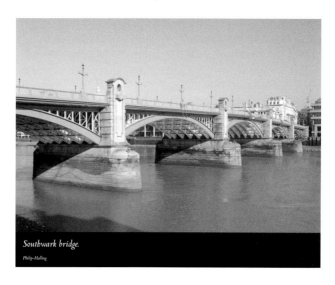

Southwark bridge.
Philip-Halling

the one-penny toll which travellers of the time would have to pay in order to cross the Thames at this point. On the south end of the bridge, one can find the Globe Theatre, a reproduction of a 17th-century playhouse famous for associations with the playwright William Shakespeare. This area was also home to bear pits, where the grisly sport of bear-baiting took place. Henry VIII promoted this activity in an effort to stamp out prostitution by abolishing brothels, known at the time as 'stew houses'. Not only were animals subject in savage fights for their lives, with hounds being pitted against bears, spectators were often maimed or killed when one of the bears broke free from the arena. Nearby Bear Gardens and Bear Alley are reminders of this form of entertainment, which was made illegal in 1835.

LONDON ODDITIES

Fancy Hats

John Hetherington was a haberdasher. That is, he made hats for all and sundry to wear while out strolling through London town. Like many modern designers of fashionable attire, Hetherington was for his time considered to be an eccentric, pushing the boundaries of headgear, so much so that in 1797 one of his headpieces caused a riot. He had spent ten months creating the world's first top hat. Upon donning the item, he took it upon himself to promenade along The Strand with his new invention. Soon attracting the attention of amazed bystanders, he found himself followed by a crowd. The newspapers of the time reported that his fancy hat made women faint, caused distress to children and dogs, and even resulted in injury to a member of the public; a poor boy running errands that day had his arm broken after being trampled

by the excited mob following John and his outrageous headwear. Hetherington soon found himself in the dock and was charged with disorder for wearing 'a tall structure having a shining lustre calculated to frighten timid people'. Found guilty, he was ordered to pay £50 costs and ordered to show more respect to public decency.

The London Beer Flood

It surely is every man's dream to find themselves engulfed in gallons of free beer, but in 1849 this was more of a nightmare. On 17 October in the Parish of St Giles, a large vat containing 135,000 gallons of the beverage burst at the Meux and Company brewery, located on Tottenham Court Road. The escaping liquid caused two adjacent vats to break, and soon a tsunami of 320,000 gallons of beer was sweeping through London. The brewery, two houses and the Tavistock Arms pub were destroyed with employee Eleanor Cooper being the first casualty of this disaster, when she was crushed in the rubble of a collapsing building. With the brewery located among the poor housing of the St Giles Rookery, the gushing torrent of beer quickly filled several basement rooms

which housed families at the time. Eight souls drowned in this flood of biblical proportions. The brewery pleaded that the disaster was an Act of God and was successful in denying its responsibility for the flood.

Dirty Dick's

Dirty Dick's pub stands on Bishopsgate Street, and had quite a reputation for being filthy; filled with dust-covered clutter, curiosities and cobwebs, and, rather disturbingly, the mummified remains of cats and rats. The pub has very much cleaned up its act and makes for a charming venue for a pint, although the cats and a few other items from the bizarre collection are still on display. It is said that these belonged to an 18th-century man named Nathaniel Bentley, who became a recluse after his fiancée died on the day before their wedding. Shutting himself away in the room where their wedding breakfast was laid, he would let nobody in, and remained there for another fifty years until his death. Bentley was rather fond of cats, so when any of them died he just kept

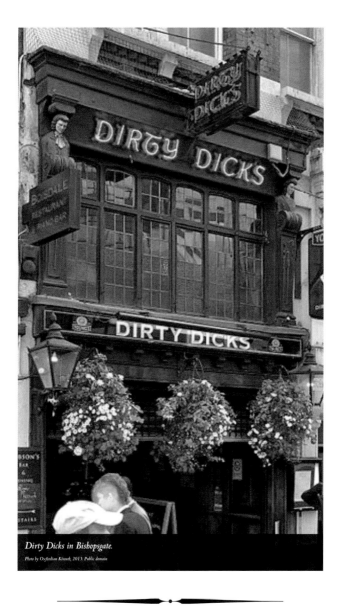

Dirty Dicks in Bishopsgate.
Photo by Oxfordian Kissuth, 2013. Public domain

them in the room with him. After he died, the tankards, rats and cats, were moved to the pub, most likely for publicity. One of the mummified cats was rigged with a spring, which would cause it to give a lifelike leap when visitors were invited to stroke the macabre remains for luck.

A Widow's Son of Bromley by Bow

by Harold Adshead

> *A widow had an only son,*
> *The sea was his concern,*
> *His parting wish an Easter Bun*
> *Be kept for his return.*
> *But when it came to Eastertide*
> *No sailor came her way*
> *To claim the bun she set aside*
> *Against the happy day.*
> *They say the ship was lost at sea,*
> *The son came home no more*
> *But still with humble piety*
> *The widow kept her store.*
> *So year by year a humble bun*
> *Was charm against despair,*
> *A loving task that once began*
> *Became her livelong care.*
> *The Widow's Son is now an inn*
> *That stands upon the site*
> *And signifies its origin*
> *Each year by Easter rite*

The buns hang up for all to see,
A blackened mass above,
A truly strange epitome
Of patient mother love.

Lucky Buns

At Bromley-by-Bow in the London district of Tower Hamlets, a pub named the Widow's Son can be found. It is famous for a vast number of stale hot cross buns suspended from the ceiling, and a new one is added to the collection every Easter on Good Friday. Folklore tells how a widow, devoted to her only son, promised to keep a hot cross bun aside for him so that he could enjoy it on returning from a voyage. He never returned, and was presumed lost at sea. His mother never gave up her hope that he would return safely, and would set one bun aside for him each year. On her death the neighbours hung all of the buns from the ceiling, and the house was named Bun Cottage before later becoming a pub. It is more likely that this collection was amassed from the belief that saving one hot cross bun each Easter would bring good luck, as a fairly common practice around England on Good Friday is to save one of these seasonal treats and preserve them somewhere dry for the whole year; replacing it with a new one twelve months later.

Wife Selling

It was once a widely held belief that a husband could legally end his marriage by selling his wife to another man. An example of such an act took place in Portman Square in the City of Westminster, as reported in *The Times* on 4 July 1833. The husband had led his wife into the market square, with a halter around her neck, symbolising that she was livestock to be sold that day. The article describes the proceedings:

> 'The business commenced amid the Hissings and booings of the populace, who showered stones and other missiles on the parties. The first bidding was 4s, and the next 4s 6d, after which an interval elapsed, amid the call of "Going, going" from the auctioneer. At last a dustman stepped forward, and exclaimed, "I wool give five bob." The woman was "knocked down" for the sum, and the dustman carried her off, nothing loth, amidst the hisses of the crowd.'

Although not entirely legal, wife selling at markets seems to have been a fairly common practice, with auctions recorded taking place all over England since the mid-16th century.

The Demon Barber

Popularised by film and television, the legend of Sweeney Todd is well known. In a courtyard off Fleet Street, Todd ran a barber's shop offering shaves and haircuts for London's gentlemen. From time to time, a wealthy customer would be preyed upon by this foul murderer; Todd would tilt the chair and they would fall down a chute into the cellar below and have their throats slit and valuables stolen. Todd's accomplice, a Mrs Lovett of Bell Yard, would then utilise the meat in her pies and sell them to the public for consumption. The crimes were eventually discovered in 1801, whereupon Todd was hanged and Lovett poisoned herself in prison.

Buried Alive

At St Giles Church in Cripplegate a poor woman was nearly buried alive in the 19th century. She had fallen into a coma and, believing her to be dead, her family arranged her funeral. Buried in a white gown, she was laid in her coffin, along with a gold wedding ring around her finger. The church sexton, a dishonest fellow, noticed this valuable ring and decided that he would take it. Returning after the funeral at night, he dug up the freshly laid earth, opened up the coffin and began to attempt to twist the ring off her cold finger. Failing in his attempt, he resolved to cut the finger off to retrieve the ring, and taking his pocket knife began to make his incision. This act roused the woman from her coma and she awoke in shock, sitting up with a scream and causing the sexton to flee in terror. The unfortunate woman shambled back home, much to the alarm of her maid who believed her to be an apparition before they realised she was indeed alive. Reunited with her family the woman went on to live a long life and had four more children. This story follows a common theme throughout the British Isles, describing a fear of being buried alive.

The Black Swine of Hampstead Sewers

In the district of Hampstead Heath, there were among the men there a few who would traverse the vast sewers searching for lost items such as money, scrap metal or jewellery, commonly known as 'tosh'. Referred to as 'shore-men' or 'toshers', these treasure-seekers were among London's poor who eked out an existence on the waste of the city that made men's fortunes. Stories emerged from the toshers of a race of wild hogs that dwelt within these sewers, in vast numbers, voracious and aggressive. The *Daily Telegraph* reported in 1859 that:

'It has been said that beasts of the chase still roam in verdant fastness of Grosvenor Square, that there are undiscovered patches of primeval forest in Hyde Park, and that Hampstead sewers shelter a monstrous breed of black swine.'

It may well be that the myth was an invention by the toshers to keep invaders out of their territory and allow them to carry on with their treasure-hunting in peace. Stories of vicious rats that would swarm over men and leave nothing left but bones were also circulated, capturing the imagination of the public. Even to this day, stories of giant rats living in London's sewers still make the newspapers, although the black swine seem to have been forgotten.

The Treasure of Camlet Moat

In Trent Park, Enfield, the stagnant Camlet Moat encircles what looks to be an island. However, it is actually the site of a manor house, which would have stood in the middle of this protective body of water. Long since gone, the house was the site of the home of Sir Geoffrey de Mandeville, Earl of Essex during the

Camlet Moat, photo by James Cridland, 2008.

Public domain

12th century. Legend tells how there is an ancient well in the north-east corner with a false bottom, underneath which is hidden a great treasure. The lost wealth of the de Mandevilles is said to be locked away in an iron chest, yet any attempts to recover it have met with failure; the chest inevitably falls right back to the bottom of the moat just before retrieval, protected by 'Wicked Sir Geoffrey' who guards his treasure from those wishing to steal it away from him.

London's Wells

Straddling the Thames, one would think there is a plentiful supply of fresh water in London. However the waters of the river are saline due to its proximity to the sea, making the water undrinkable. Throughout the city, wells could be found, providing a plentiful source of clean, clear spring water.

In times when disease was rife and dirty water a cause of sickness, these wells were often attributed with miraculous healing qualities, as those who drank from them seldom became ill. We now know of course that this is because the waters were unpolluted by sewerage or other contamination, but the people of old would dedicate their wells to saints or in pre-Christian times, other deities, treating the wells as shrines for the gifts they bestowed upon the people. Many of these wells have now been lost over the years due to development of the city. Some of them can still be found hidden throughout London.

Wells throughout the British Isles were often seen to be sacred, and certainly associations with the goddess Brigid are common, especially in Ireland. She was associated with childbirth, lambing, fire, and water, libations left in her honour such as crosses crafted from reeds. In Christian times, Brigid was transformed into a saint and her veneration continued. There are many variations on her name, Bride being one of them. St. Bride's Well on Fleet Street was sited alongside an ancient well, and it is speculated that this site was originally a shrine to the earlier goddess and was a source of clean water right up until the 19th Century.

Beneath the Australian High Commission Building on the Strand, a well with waters crisp and clear can be found, hidden beneath a manhole cover. The well had been used for centuries before being covered, and was known to Anglo-Saxon and Norman inhabitants of the area. Originally sited on Holywell Street, this spring was lost to the public during the late 19th Century during works to clear the city's slums. It is believed that this well is Holy Well, described by John Stowe in his 1698 Survey of London as being "much decayed and marred with filthiness purposely laid there, for the heightening of the ground for garden-plots". Stowe's description could instead apply to Holywell, thought to be somewhere beneath the district of Shoreditch.

Near to the Australian Embassy, another well was sited at the church of St. Clement Danes. Folklore around the site describes how the Danes had settled in Aldwych outside the walls of the City of London and had built a church dedicated to St. Clement, the Patron Saint of Mariners. An alternative story explains that Anglo-Saxon King Alfred the Great had built the church after evicting the Danes from London, to give thanks to god, with another tale describing how the church was built in memory of a great number of Danes massacred at the site. What we can be sure of is that it is likely that the well was considered sacred long before a church was built on the spot.

Another surviving well can be seen through the floor at the Salder's Well theatre in Isington, covered by a sheet of glass. Originally established by Richard Salder in 1683 as a Music House and pleasure garden, the springs were believed to possess miraculous

Sadler's Wells, as it was in 1737, with fashionable water-drinkers.
Wellcome Library, Public domain

Sadler's Wells.
Philip Vile. Courtesy of Sadler's Wells

'She Ran to St Govor's Well and Hid' by Arthur Rackham, 1906. From *Peter Pan in Kensington Gardens* by J. M. Barrie.

qualities and Sadler was keen to promote these to encourage visitors. It was claimed that "dropsy, jaundice, scurvy, green sickness and other distempers to which females are liable – ulcers, fits of the mother, virgin's fever and hyperchondriacal distemper" could be treated by drinking water from the well.

Kensington Gardens was the site of two wells. Mentioned in Peter Pan by J. M. Barrie, St. Govor's well is now marked by a fountain, whilst St. Agnes' well has disappeared. St Agnes is among other things, the patron saint of gardens, so one can speculate that the well at Kensington influenced the creation of the gardens we can still enjoy to this day.

Good Luck, Bad Luck

According to our London ancestors, if you want to ensure good luck then DO:

Utter 'Waste not want not, pick it up and eat it' upon finding a discarded morsel; then you could eat it without suffering any harm.

Cover up mirrors and water jugs at the first sign of a thunderstorm to avoid being struck by lightning.

According to our London ancestors, if you want to avoid bad luck then DON'T:

Pick up a cut flower lying on the ground, as it would mean that you would pick up a fever.

Tread on the cracks between paving stones as it would bring an accident.

Cross two knives; it would result in a row.

Drop a spoon; an unwelcome visitor will soon attend or bad news will come.

Folk Remedies

City life brought with it many illnesses, and the pollution of London's streets caused misery and death for countless numbers of its residents. Densely populated and often living in cramped conditions, disease was rife. To grant some protection from disease, in particular bronchitis, a necklace of beads was put around the necks of infants, never to be taken off, even when washed or bathed. Not even at death were these removed, and should a necklace break it would at once be rethreaded on a fresh string. Edward Lovett described in *Magic in Modern London* how at times the colours could vary, with dark blue, yellow or white beads sometimes being used, but the predominant colour would be sky blue. It is not known where this custom originated, although in Greece and Turkey blue glass is also believed to have protective powers. Like many superstitions of the city, this custom may have been brought in by merchants, or may have even older origins from Anglo-Saxon or Roman times.

Plague outbreaks were a constant fear in any city, and London was no exception, with a particularly unpleasant outbreak taking place in 1665 which killed an estimated quarter of the city's population. Small posies or bags containing flowers were carried. These were known as nosegays, and it was believed that the sweet fragrances masking the stink of the filthy city streets would protect the wearer from disease. Chewing a dried angelica root was also recommended. Should a person become infected, then an animal – living or dead – might be used to draw out the poison. One such remedy from the 16th century, claiming to be 'a medison that the Lord maier had from the queen which is a most presious medison for the plague and much aproved', describes taking a 'cocke chicken or a pullet and set the rumpe to the sore'.

Despite the paved streets and crowded buildings, there was space for small gardens around London, more so than today. Plots would be used for small kitchen gardens, with sections set aside by some to grow medicinal herbs. With doctors being expensive, many relied on the local wise woman to help with illnesses and injuries, from broken bones and bad coughs to delivering babies. It was believed that plants displayed their healing attributes through their appearances. For example, lungwort, with its spotted leaves which reminded herbalists of pulmonary disease, was chosen to treat chest complaints. Should someone be suffering from jaundice, with its noticeable yellowing of the skin, plants with yellow flowers, or yellow spices, would be used to treat the illness, such as a concoction of turmeric and saffron mixed together in white wine. Throughout the ages the names given to plants were chosen to help us easily remember what they were good for. Indeed many of our recipes seem to have been created with some medicinal benefit intended. Sage, for example, is known to be good for digestion, so it is no surprise to find it as an ingredient of stuffing, which is served with rich meats to prevent indigestion.

It was Nicholas Culpeper, practising in Spitalfields in the early 17th century, who catalogued the medicinal and astrological properties of many of these herbs and other plants in his famous book of 1653, the *Complete Herbal*. Certain remedies described by Culpeper include anemone as a juice to clean ulcerations, treat infections, cure leprosy and clear the nostrils, the sap of milkweed for removing warts, and mugwort for use in inducing labour and easing labour pains. Culpeper was not only interested in medicine; he studied astrology and worked with William Lilly.

LONDON CALENDAR CUSTOMS

6 January – *Baddeley Cake*

The tradition of serving cake and wine on Twelfth Night at Drury Lane's Theatre Royal began in 1794 following the death of actor Robert Baddeley. While Baddeley Cake is a well-known custom in acting circles, this tradition is a private affair and is not open to the general public.

6 January – *Twelfth Night at Bankside*

Near the Globe Theatre on the banks of the Thames, mummers and wassailers join the Holly Man to celebrate Twelfth Night. The traditions of mumming and wassailing at wintertime in Britain are believed to have origins in the ancient history of this nation. The Holly Man, dressed in evergreens, arrives by boat from the Thames accompanied by his merry men. Dancing to Bankside, the mummers' play of the death and resurrection of St George takes place. At the end of the play, cakes are passed around the audience, and those who find a concealed pea and bean within their cakes are crowned the King and Queen for the day. The group then makes its way to the George Inn on Borough High Street for more merriment and singing.

Nearest Sunday after 6 January — *The Blessing of the River Thames*

Each January, the Thames is blessed by the clergy of South Bank's Southwark Cathedral and North Bank's Church of St Magnus the Martyr, who meet halfway on London Bridge. Prayers are said, after which a wooden cross is cast into the swirling waters. The tradition of throwing a cross into the river is believed to have its origins with the Orthodox Church, who would hold a service and throw a cross into the river the Sunday after Epiphany (Twelfth Night).

30 January — *The Charles I Commemoration*

King Charles I was publicly executed on 30 January 1649 for High Treason after refusing the demands of the Oliver Cromwell and his Parliamentarians for a constitutional monarchy. A statue was erected outside the Banqueting Hall in Whitehall marking the spot where the king was decapitated, and each year The Society of King Charles the Martyr remembers him with prayers and wreath laying at the statue.

First Sunday in February — *The Clowns Service*

A service for clowns is held at All Saints Church in Hackney, to commemorate the life of Joseph Grimaldi, London's most celebrated clown who was born in 1778. Grimaldi died on 31 May 1837, and a service for these colourful entertainers has taken place ever since. The congregation dresses in their full clown costumes, and props such as dusters and honking horns often feature.

3 February — *Holborn Blessing of the Throats*

The feast day of St Blaise, patron saint of Woolcombers, is celebrated at St Etheldreda's Church in Holborn on 3rd or occasionally 4th February. Woolcombers would be prone to suffering maladies of the throat thanks to the fine barbs within the wool which they inhaled during their daily labour.

Shrove Tuesday – *The London Inter Livery Pancake Race*

Shrove Tuesday is the day before the start of Lent and falls in February or March each year depending on the date on which Easter Sunday is celebrated. The Worshipful Company of Poulters was formed to regulate poultry, swans, rabbits, pigeons and small game in medieval times. The Company now operates as a charitable institution and organises an annual pancake race at noon at the Guildhall Yard on Gresham Street, inviting the other Worshipful Companies of London to participate. The teams each play a specific part in the celebration, with the starting gun fired by the Worshipful Company of Gunmakers, lemons supplied by the Worshipful Company of Fruiterers, the Worshipful Company of Cutlers providing plastic forks, and the Worshipful Company of Poulters providing the eggs for the pancake mix. The whole race is timed by the Clerk of the Worshipful Company of Clockmakers, while the participants race wearing white gloves provided by the Worshipful Company of Glovers, while musically accompanied by the tuneful voices of the Musicians' Company. Funds raised from this event are donated to the Lord Mayor's Charity.

End of February, start of March – *The Trial of the Pyx*

Each year, the Freemen of the Goldsmiths' Company choose a date upon which to inspect coins produced by the Royal Mint. A pyx (a container used by the Royal Mint for holding specimen coins) is filled with a selection of coins which are weighed and counted and are then sent off to test the purities of their composition. The Company will then reconvene some weeks later to discuss their findings and attend a luncheon. Both events are private and are not open to the public.

Third Tuesday in March – *Oranges and Lemons Service*

Oranges and lemons,
Say the bells of St Clement's.

You owe me five farthings,
Say the bells of St Martin's.

When will you pay me?
Say the bells of Old Bailey.

When I grow rich,
Say the bells of Shoreditch.

When will that be?
Say the bells of Stepney.

I do not know,
Says the great bell of Bow.

Here comes a candle to light you to bed,
And here comes a chopper to chop off your head!

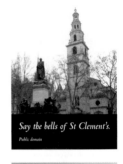

Say the bells of St Clement's.
Public domain

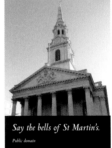

Say the bells of St Martin's.
Public domain

This popular children's nursery rhyme features the bells of many of London's churches, and is celebrated each year at the church of St Clement Danes, which holds an Oranges and Lemons service. Following the re-hanging of the church bells in 1919, this service is themed towards local children, although all are welcome to attend. Oranges and lemons are blessed and handed out to the children of the congregation to take home with them, marking the historical association of St Clements which once charged a toll to ships carrying cargoes of fruit up the Thames.

Say the bells of Old Bailey.
Public domain

Say the bells of Shoreditch.
Public domain

Say the bells of Stepney.
Public domain

Say the bells of Bow.
Public domain

Good Friday — *London Butterworth Charity and Widow's Sixpence*

Good Friday marks the day in the Christian calendar when Jesus was martyred on the cross. The date varies based on when Easter falls in a particular year. A tradition on this day was to hand out a dole to the poor, and the parish of St Bartholomew the Great would give food and a sixpence to poor widows. To this day, hot cross buns are handed out in the churchyard, while the Widow's Sixpence is available to any poor widow who attends the service. Since the sixpence piece is no longer in circulation, this now equates to 20p!

Easter Monday — *Greenwich Easter Lifting*

It was once a common tradition around England to hold a Heaving or Lifting ceremony on the first Monday after Easter Sunday. Blackheath Morris have carried the torch with this custom, arranging a Lifting as their first Outing of the year. A chair is decorated with flowers, and women are invited to take a seat. They are lifted three times and spun around, before the men demand their reward of a kiss. This custom was met in the past with disapproval from the Church as it is rumoured to have ancient origins, either as a fertility rite or as a parody of the resurrection of Jesus Christ.

Late April, early May — *The Tudor Pull*

Said to have its origins with celebrations commemorating the sinking of Queen Eleanor's barge near London Bridge in 1256, this rowing event takes place each year on a Sunday on the River Thames. The flotilla's 25-mile trip begins at the Royal Palace at Hampton Court to deliver a 'stela' (a piece of wooden water pipe) to the Governor of the Tower of London. Decked out in bright livery, the fleet includes a Royal Barge, the flotilla of the Thames Watermen's cutters, clippers and rowing boats. Quite a sight to behold in modern-day London.

I May – *The May Day Sweep*

Chimney Sweep's Day, Blackbird is gay,

Here he is singing, you see, in the May.

He has feathers as black as a chimney sweep's coat.

So on Chimney Sweeps' Day he must pipe a glad note.

I May – *Jack-in-the-Green*

Jack-in-the-Green from door to door

Capers along with his followers four.

As May Day mummers are seldom seen,

Let us all give a copper to Jack-in-the-Green.

May Day is celebrated throughout the British Isles, with maypole dances and fetes held to welcome the arrival of nature's bounty to the lands. The City of London and the areas of Brentham and Deptford hold a carnival whereby a troop of Morris Men known as a Fowlers Troop lead 'Jack' through the streets to music, dancing and much merriment. Dressed from head to toe in green foliage, Jack is led by celebrants to a place where he is symbolically slain to release the spirit of summer. Jack is associated with the much older mythical figures of the Green Man, Puck and Robin Goodfellow.

18th century illustration of Jack-in-the-Green, London.
Wellcome Library, Public domain

Ascension Day (every 3 years) – *The London Beating the Bounds with Battle*

Ascension Day is another moveable feast and takes place on the fortieth day after Easter Sunday. In days long past members of a parish would walk the boundaries to make sure that their boundary markers had not been moved by adjacent landowners. This practice is believed to have begun in the times of the Anglo-Saxons. The London Beating the Bounds is observed by All Hallows by the Tower and the Tower of London. While the All Hallows Beating the Bounds takes place every year, that of the Tower of London takes place only once every three years. The Tower's Beating Party includes a procession of Yeomen Warders and the Gaoler complete with his axe. Accompanied by children who are given willow wands, the Chief Yeoman Warder orders them to strike each of the 31 markers along their boundary with a cry of 'Whack it boys, whack it!'

Late May, early June – *The Knollys Rose Ceremony*

In 1381 Lady Constance Knollys built a footbridge between two of her properties on Seething Lane without permission. For this she was fined one red rose. This strange and rather beautiful punishment has been honoured as a custom by the Company of Watermen and lightermen of the River Thames, where a rose is chosen and cut from the gardens of All Hallows Church and is carried on a velvet cushion to the Lord Mayor at Mansion House. The date varies but the ceremony tends to take place on a weekday in early June.

Second Wednesday in July – *Procession of the Worshipful Company of Vintners*

One of the City of London's Worshipful Companies, the Vintners were once responsible for the quality and trade of wine within the City. Each year they elect a new Master, and a procession is held from the Vintners' Hall on Upper Thames Street to the Church of St James Garlickhythe where the Master and Company take part in a service.

Mid July – *The Doggett's Coat and Badge Wager*

Founded in 1715 by Thomas Doggett, this contest is claimed to be the oldest rowing race in the world. An Irishman, Doggett was a joint manager of the Drury Lane Theatre where he performed as an actor and comedian. There were not as many bridges across the Thames as we see these days, and so watermen would carry passengers across the river. The story goes that in 1715 Doggett fell overboard while crossing the Thames near Embankment and was rescued by the Fishmongers' Company. In gratitude of his being saved, he offered a wager of a red watermen's coat to the fastest six watermen. The four and-a-half mile rowing race continues each year, between London Bridge and Cadogan Pier at Chelsea, with the red coat being awarded to the winner.

Third Week of July – *Swan Upping*

A regal and elegant bird, the swans that live on the Thames belong to the Sovereign and to the Worshipful Companies of Dyers and Vintners who were granted this privilege in the 15th century. A census takes place each year during July, in which the birds were traditionally counted and marked to show who they belonged to. One nick in the beak showed that it was the property of the Dyers Company. Two nicks, it belonged to the Vintners. No nicks at all, it would belong to the Crown ruler of England. In modern times, the ceremony is used to carry out a census and check the health of these birds, and tend to any that are sick or injured. Instead of having their beaks marked, they are instead tagged or ringed. The swan markers still wear their traditional livery, and travel up the Thames in skiffs bearing the flags of their Company or the Sovereign.

Last Sunday of September – *London Bridge Sheep Drive*

In medieval London, London Bridge was the only bridge crossing the Thames and a toll was charged to anyone wishing to cross it and enter the City. While merchants would have to pay taxes to the City for trading within its walls, the toll was waived for those with the status of Freeman of the City of London and included the right for traders to bring their tools into the City. This was a valuable economic privilege to the merchants and craftsmen of those times. To demonstrate their right to exemption from tolls, members of the Worshipful Company of Woolmen would drive their sheep across the bridge each year. Founded in 1880, this group is one of the oldest Livery Companies of London.

Last Sunday of September – *Costermongers' Harvest Festival*

A costermonger was the name used to describe someone who sold goods from a wheeled cart in the street, usually fruit and vegetables but sometimes other items. This was often the livelihood of the Cockney Londoner, and on the last Sunday of September this heritage is celebrated with a harvest festival. London's dazzlingly decorated Pearly Kings and Queens turn out en masse at the church of St Mary-le-Bow at Cheapside. Their costumes of black, adorned with buttons are distinctive and extravagant, and are believed to have been inspired by the invention of Henry Croft, a road-sweeper who was inspired by the way in which costermongers decorated their clothing. The afternoon has a carnival atmosphere with singing and dancing from morris dancers watched by red-coated Chelsea pensioners in the Guildhall Yard. The Pearly Kings and Queens lead the show with traditional Cockney songs and a good old-fashioned knees-up, while the Bow Bells are rung. A noisy and colourful affair, it really is a must-see for anyone eager to witness a lively and authentic slice of London culture.

Pearly Kings and Queens collecting for charity at London's Covent Garden.

Photo by Garry Knight, Wellcome Library, Public domain

First Sunday in October – *The Covent Garden Punch and Judy Festival*

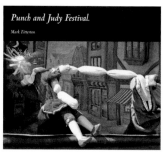

Punch and Judy Festival.

Mark Titterton

Perhaps this festival is in danger of dying out, as it was last held in 2012. Each year puppeteers would set up booths near the Punch and Judy pub and give performances. Known as Professors, the practitioners would celebrate what is said to be the birthplace of the Punch and Judy show. It is said that Samuel Pepys was the first to record a puppet performance here, when he wrote in a diary entry of Friday 9 May, 1662:

'Thence with Mr Salisbury, who I met there, into Covent Garden to an alehouse, to see a picture that hangs there, which is offered for 20s., and I offered fourteen — but it is worth much more money — but did not buy it, I having no mind to break my oath. Thence to see an Italian puppet play that is within the rayles there, which is very pretty, the best that I ever saw, and a great resort of gallants.'

21 October – *Trafalgar Day*

Held at St Paul's Cathedral and in Trafalgar Square, each year a gathering occurs to celebrate Admiral Lord Nelson's victory at the Battle of Trafalgar in 1805.

Mid November – *The Lord Mayor's Show*

The oldest civic procession in the world, this event has taken place each year for over 800 years. Every November, the newly elected Mayor makes his way from Mansion House to pledge allegiance to the Crown at the Royal Courts of Justice on the Strand.

31 December – *New Year's Eve*

New Year's celebrations around England include staying up to see in the New Year. A beloved part of this tradition is to listen to the chimes of Big Ben strike midnight. While many consider the clock and tower to be called Big Ben, this name is actually specific to the bell itself, with the tower named The Elizabeth Tower. Traditions around New Year include the making of resolutions to improve one's life in the coming year, and also the opening of the back door and front door to blow the bad luck out of the house and welcome the New Year in.

Other London books for you to enjoy

**Order from your local bookshop
or online at bradwellbooks.co.uk**

Cockney Dialect: A Selection of
Words and Anecdotes from the East
End of London
ISBN 9781902674643

London Ghost Stories
ISBN 9781909914384

London Murder Stories
ISBN 9781910551769

London Underground Ghost Stories
ISBN 9781902674711

London Wit & Humour
ISBN 9781909914445

Walks for All Ages Greater London
ISBN 9781910551097

**Other Legends & Folklore books
for you to enjoy**

Legends & Folklore Cambridgeshire
ISBN 9781910551486

Legends & Folklore Cornwall
ISBN 9781912060696

Legends & Folklore Dorset
ISBN 9781910551493

Legends & Folklore Hampshire
ISBN 9781910551509

Legends & Folklore Nottinghamshire
ISBN 9781909914971

Legends & Folklore Scotland
ISBN 9781909914988

Legends & Folklore Somerset
ISBN 9781910551516

Legends & Folklore the Peak District
ISBN 9781912060702

Legends & Folklore Wales
ISBN 9781909914995

Legends & Folklore Wiltshire
ISBN 9781910551004

Legends & Folklore Yorkshire
ISBN 9781912060719